Food for Saints

By

Dr. Lydia A. Woods

†††
CWP

Channing and Watt Publishers
Atlanta, GA

Food for Saints, Copyright © 1997 Lydia A. Woods

All rights reserved.

Channing and Watt Publishers
75 Gammon Ave SE Apt #A
Atlanta, Georgia 30315
www.channingandwatt.com

Front Cover Photo and Cover Design by
Jacqueline D. Woods/JD Woods Consulting

Back Cover Photo by
Elizabeth J. Jackson

First Edition, Copyright © 1997 Lydia A. Woods
Second Edition, Copyright © 2014 Lydia A. Woods

Printed in the United States of America

ISBN-13: 978-1-941200-15-5
LCCN: 2001088527

Other Publications
by Dr. Lydia A. Woods

Dedicated to
Watt and Woods Women
Ruth, Genevieve, Vera, Mildred,
Jacqueline and Valerie

Acknowledgements

A piece of creative work is usually produced in isolation, but the distribution for others to see and appreciate takes many hearts and hands and minds. I want to give thanks to my friends and family members who are those hearts which support and lift me up and forward.

Special thanks to William C. Terry, Yehonatan Meru, and Veronica Norris for taking their time to proofread this book.

My appreciation to the host of colleagues, students and fellow Christian brothers and sisters who praise and encourage me and constantly remind me of the work God can do in a willing but frightened and fragile vessel.

Thank you Holy Spirit for using my humble vessel
and letting me put my name on these words.

Introduction

Under the inspiration of the Holy Spirit, I began writing Christian Poetry. When I look back at the beginning, I realize now that I knew very little about the Holy Spirit and His relationship to me. At first, I would be awakened during the night, out of a sound sleep, with a poem forming in my head, or sometimes while driving, or in the midst of conversation with someone.

I would tell people that the Spirit would come and go, then months later return, to give me poems. My understanding has since grown, and I now know that the Spirit never leaves and is always present with me and in me and thru me – the two of us are one.

I believe the Holy Spirit, is God and that God exists in every human being. The real gift of life is discovering God within you, which first blesses you, then those around you.

These collections of poems are inspired by the lessons which the Lord has been teaching me as I walk with Him. Many poems are inspired by uplifting and stimulating conversations with God's precious Saints and others are born out of the frustration that many do not know the Love of God and His amazing grace and mercy.

In reading, I hope you will find poems which speak to your heart, express what you have experienced, or have enlightened your understanding. The writing of these poems allow me an outlet of spiritual expression, as the Lord tempers and prepares me for my Calling..

Table of Contents

Poems

Scriptural References

Poems

Dr. Lydia A. Woods

Above All

John 14:13; I John 5:14; Ephesians 3:10 (KJV)

Why is it written that He will do,
Above all that we ask Him to?

Also above that which we can think, also,
I've often wondered about this, I want to know.

I've figured out that He's placed every desire in my heart,
That it did not originate on my small part.

The Lord placed those desires so long ago,
Before I was born in fact – didn't you know?

So if He has placed those desires there,
He is also able to fulfill them with love and care.

But He holds a little back for Himself,
To surprise His children and bless them with His wealth.

That's the part about "Above All," that we can think or ask,
He saves the extra special part until the very last.

He has wealth, that even our minds can't comprehend,
And He likes to play the "Above Card," in the end.

He enjoys seeing our joy and delight,
It makes our testimony glorious and extraordinarily bright.

We can't wait to tell just what He has done,
We want to run and share it with everyone.

That He didn't just do, what we had asked,
But He went beyond that wee small task.

He never does things tiny or infinitely small,
But He is in the business of – Above All!

Be Still!

Psalm 46:10 (KJV)

As a child of God, He often says to me,
Child "Be Still," just wait and see.
I hate it when He says, "Be Still,"
Cause' my flesh is jumpin' – that's against my will.

He means, "Be Still," in your flesh and mouth and mind,
Just sit yourself down on your behind.

The nature of a child is to move, move about,
Running here and there trying to figure things out.
Just what to do about this and that,
That's true about kids and that is just a fact.

So when the Father says to "Be Still,"
He means that we are to submit our Will,
The very thing that you want to do,
Put it on the shelf, like He told you to.

He has a plan for the problem already in hand,
Before you were born, because He "Is the Man,"
In heaven and earth it's always His Will,
So will you just sit down and "Be Still!"

Children of the King

I John 3:1, 9; Psalm 91:11; Matthew 4:6 (KJV)

Do you really know how the children of Kings are treated?
They are waited on hand-and-foot while they are seated.

And when they get up to walk about,
The servants clear a path without a doubt.

Preparation is always being made on their behalf,
They are never far from the king's rod or staff.

Maybe the example of "Children of Kings," is too far out for you,
Let me bring it closer to home for your review.

Now the President of the United States has secret service guys,
And what is their purpose? – I will tell you why.

They are sent before to scout out the situation,
To make sure it's safe, posting men at every station.

Undercover secret service are everywhere,
Assassins watch out – you are stupid if you dare,

To attack the President would not be very wise.
It's a crazy scary plan that I would not advise.

'Cause the secret service will be on you, like white on rice,
They won't treat you kindly or handle you very nice.

The President is important and special indeed,
For the nation to function and thrive and succeed.

And God's children are special and important in this dark hour,
He plans for us to succeed, as we walk with pride and power.

Now imagine, that your secret service people are on the job,
Get a sense that what I'm saying isn't so very odd.

Our undercover agents are Angels you know,
They are around you and above you - wherever you go.

They've been assigned by the Father to protect His child,
Keeping you guarded and safe on earth, all the while.

Surely goodness and mercy will follow you all of your days,
This is just another example of our loving Father's ways.

Get a revelation – blessed children of the King,
Begin to walk with pride and boldness into Anything!

Doin' the Adam

Genesis 3:1-24 (KJV)

Now I want you to check Genesis out,
Because everyone seems to believe,
That Adam was away in the garden,
Not standing beside his wife Eve.

When the serpent began his conversation,
Lying and twisting God's Holy Word.
Tempting Eve of the fruit to partake,
The whole conversation Adam surely heard.

It was Adam that God gave dominion,
Over the earth and every living new birth,
All he needed to say to the serpent was,
Be gone – I cast you out from the earth.

But he abdicated his authority,
He sold his very birthright,
His power over the earth was given to Satan,
Now Satan ruled over Adam and his wife.

They lost their glorified bodies,
They became subject to death that day,
This hindered their relationship with God,
Because they listened to what Satan had to say.

Why did he not use his authority?
Why did he stand stupidly by?
Did he not understand his commission, from the Lord?
Can anyone tell me why?

And if you can tell why Adam,
Committed that sin long ago,
Then you can probably tell me why Saints today,
Are doin' the Adam and don't seem to know,

That God carried out a glorious plan,
To restore us to Himself through His Son.
Giving all power back in the hands of the Saints,
By the victory that Jesus won.

So don't be caught doin' the Adam,
I see Saints falling for Satan's old familiar song,
Don't stand stupidly by and listen,
Remember – Adam's mistake, now make right the wrong!

Father Knows Best

Proverbs 1:7; James 1:5 (KJV)

"Father Knows Best," was the name of a television show,
I know I'm dating myself, but some of you know.

The wife and kids would get themselves in a stew,
But the wise Father always knew just what to do.

I know you've heard that where there's a will – there is a way.
I just want to discuss that old saying with you today.

For where our Will is, I only know there is a mess,
'Cause only the Will of the Father is the One that's best.

We try very hard to have our own way,
Telling God how it's going to be today.

Strutting around with our chests poked out,
We even have a nerve to get mad or pout.

But you know just what I'm talking about,
Look at your life the proof will bear me out.

That our will is the source of all the hurt and pain,
It has screwed us up – it can drive us insane.

I know that my will has got to lay down and die,
But it keeps getting up and this is why,

'Cause that will has been trained by the evil one,
To rebel against God and His precious Son.

The greatest gift the Lord gives is our own will,
But it's a difficult thing to make it be still.

To line it up with the Lord's, is the secret of life,
And living on this earth without fear or strife.

A will submitted to Him will find joy, peace and rest,
It's for our own good, 'cause, "Father Knows Best."

Father Knows Best   *A Collection of Christian Poems*

For the Elect's Sake

Mark 13:20 (KJV)

Have you noticed that the days,
Seem shorter and shorter each year,
Before you know it the months have flown,
Everyone's talking about time – now hear,

Just what is really going on,
With the time and why is it moving with speed?
Can you not discern the signs of the times,
Lend an ear to God's Word, give heed.

We are definitely in the last days,
Prophecy is fulfilling itself as I speak,
The spirit of antichrist is fully in season,
Many Saints today are just Spiritually weak.

He is shortening the days,
For the sake of the very Elect,
Because of the rampant sin,
In the world and the Elect doesn't really suspect,

That they are compromising God's Word,
They have a form of godliness but deny,
The power of His Name,
They are missing His commission and this is why.

They are attending church in great numbers,
Their itching ears heap teachers to themselves.
They are building great monuments and structures,
They marvel at the size of their congregations and their wealth.

But...
The Body of Christ by the Holy Spirit,
Is to be a powerful force in the world today,
But they won't take in His Holy Spirit,
That gives them power to defeat Satan in every way.

They are not walking in this power,
Doing greater things than the Lord did when He was here,
For their faith is extremely weak,
So much of the church in darkness and fear.

They fear the power of the Holy Spirit,
They won't let the gifts operate in their midst,
They are steeped in their traditions,
The ways of the Lord they resist.

Strongholds are not being broken,
People gather but none are set free.
Why do you continue to meet on Sunday
And never access the power in Me?

-12-

Bring your sick and heavy ladened,
To My altar, anoint them and lay hands in My Name,
Cast the demons out of the people,
Free their minds that Satan has claimed.

Believe in the power of My Name,
Use it boldly and never fear,
That My Word will return to Me void,
Are you listening my precious dears?

I have shortened the time for My Elect,
Satan seems to be winning, but My dears don't fear.
For those of you that are in Me,
Know that the victory is already here!

Get in the House

Exodus 12:12-14; James 2:12, 18-19 (KJV)

When you were young, outside you'd play,
And after a very long hard day.
When night was falling, mom would always say,
"Get in the House, play is over for today."

There is safety in the house when darkness falls,
So obey your mother when she calls,
Also obey the Heavenly Father's Word,
'Cause the plague is still lurking, so I've heard.

And so it was in days long ago,
The plague wandered in the streets – don't you know,
But all of Goshen land was spared,
For out the house they did not dare.

They spread the Blood above the door,
Obeyed the Father who evened the score,
With the Egyptians on that terrible day,
'Cause they didn't heed what Moses had to say.

"Let the people go," was the Father's command,
And against the Lord can no man stand,
Not even Pharaoh the mighty king,
Could save the first born from this thing.

There is salvation in the house for all inside,
It takes only one righteous for the others to abide.
That one righteous soul can cover a multitude of sin.
And win the salvation of all their house in the end.

The scriptures tell of other houses spared,
Because Noah listened to God and he did dare.
To build the Ark – then in it his family place,
And they all were saved by the Lord's good grace.

Now Rahab too made sure her family was within,
For she hid the spies and that covered her sin.
That red thread hung outside for all to see,
Symbolic of the Blood of Christ, who sets us free.

So get in the house for salvation is there,
For you and your household take special care.
You're commanded to cover it very well,
With the Lord's Blood, like a precious veil.

And He is faithful to save those gathered inside,
Never fear or fret it's for you to decide,
So remember what your mama used to say,
"Get in the House, play is over for today!"

God's M.O.

I Corinthians 1:26-27, 2:7, 3:19; Luke 2:7;Ephesians 3:5 (KJV)

My relationship with the Father,
Is growing from day to day,
I'm learning of His unique character,
And a little something about His way.

How He doesn't come right at you,
He's not in your face plain and clear.
But you need to look a little deeper,
To see what's really going on here.

How he brought His Son in low estate,
Not a King upon a throne,
He is subtle and quite ingenious,
But if you're not careful you'll go wrong.

He takes the foolishness of man,
To confound the very wise,
Those discarded things of man,
Are the Lord's greatest prize.

The very thing that doesn't appeal to you,
And makes you want to run the other way,
Give it a second deeper look,
Cause I discovered a secret one day.

-17-

That Satan comes at you like an angel of light,
Disguising the bad behind the good,
And the minute you take the bait,
That's when he pulls the hood,

And uncovers the horrible mess,
That he has sucked you in for sure,
Now you're screaming for help,
Looking to God for the problem's cure.

So don't be sucked in by outward appearances,
Listen carefully and look for God's M.O.
If it doesn't appeal to your flesh,
It's probably the way you ought to go.

So when I am just plain obedient,
Even when I don't want to obey,
I'm always fantastically blessed,
When I give in and do it God's way.

God's M.O.   *A Collection of Christian Poems*

I'm Not Lucky - I'm Blessed!

Genesis 12:3, 26:4; Deuteronomy 7:3-14 (KJV)

I tell people all the time,
I'm not lucky – I'm blessed.
Luck is a word the world uses,
But blessed is the term I prefer to confess.

Lucky is not in the vocabulary of God's Word,
Saints rid luck from your conversation today.
It's only God's grace and mercy,
That follows us as we journey in life's way.

Lucky is a term of Satan,
It involves witchcraft and chances of fate.
But promises of God's blessings to His children,
Is not magic, but a sure and solid mandate.

We live in the showering of His blessings,
We walk in grace and mercy from hour to hour,
Miracles are just everyday occurrences,
It's our birthright to live our lives in His power.

The power of His Word,
That transcends every wicked device,
There is power in our tongues,
Saints let's correct our speech, that's my advice.

Remember that it is not luck,
That comes and goes at Satan's whim,
But the state of our existence,
When we walk by Faith in Him.

I'm Tired!

John 16:33; Ephesians 5:3-5 (KJV)

My precious Saints don't pray to be released,
Calling for the debt and troubles to cease.
Stop waiting for your ship to come in,
Falling for every scam of the enemy... Satan!

You know the familiar phrases you love to hear,
"The Lord doesn't want you in poverty my dear,"
"The Lord wants you to prosper," and I have a way,
Listen to this "Prosperity message," I'm selling today.

Don't fall for Satan's old funky tricks, that crook,
He uses the Word just enough to get you hooked.
You are so desperate to be out of debt,
Saints are tired of struggling of that you can bet.

You say...

I'm tired of not having money in the bank,
I'm tired of not having a brand new car with a full tank.
I'm tired of not Traveling here and there,
I'm tired of not having fancy clothes to wear.

I'm tired of this old boring job,
I'm tired of being peculiar and thought of as odd.
I'm tired of not having what I deserve,
I'm a child of God, haven't you heard?

He wants all His children to be prosperous you see,
So I'll just pray for what I want to come to me.
I know the Lord loves me so,
This can't be His plan for my life don't you know.

The debt and pressure and stress and strain,
It's all becoming too much for my little brain,
I'm really about to lose it Lord,
Where is all the prosperity you promised in Your Word?

It's all part of His plan for us,
Debt and tribulation are for a greater purpose.
To draw you closer and closer to Himself,
Making you rely on Him and His infinite wealth.

For His children have access to a greater wealth,
The Lord wants you to learn to access it for yourself,
Now I want to say this loud and clear,
Open up your ears so that you can hear.

The Lord wants you to rely and trust in Him,
And be content no matter what state you are in.
Be content and rest in Him in joy and peace,
And only then will your constant longing cease.

It's in your contentment, that you'll come to see.
That it's never been about you or me.
That it's only been about the Father and Son,
And becoming a part of the greater One.

And you'll discover all the wealth and riches there,
That are far bigger than any worry or care.
You'll understand that this is not your home.
You'll begin to grow-up and be full grown,

In the realm of the Spirit,
Now you have come up higher,
All frustrations and fears are gone,
And in the Spirit you'll never tire!

-23-

If You Loved Me Lord...

Romans 8:26; James 4:3 (KJV)

I prayed for riches to give to the poor,
I've proved I'm a giver, so Lord, bless me with more.

I asked, but I didn't get, so what's-up with that,
If You loved me Lord, you'd give – Ain't that a fact!

I prayed continuously for a mate,
It seemed like a good thing for my sake.

I asked, but I didn't get, so what's-up with that,
If You loved me Lord, you'd give – Ain't that a fact!

My prayers never cease for my family to be saved,
But I wonder if they will, before I go to my grave.

I asked, but I didn't get, so what's-up with that,
If You loved me Lord, you'd give – Ain't that a fact!

My prayers go up daily for my poverty to end,
Pressed down, running over, you said, I'd be given to by men.

I asked, but I didn't get, so what's-up with that,
If You loved me Lord, you'd give – Ain't that a fact!

My prayers are never ending for my sickness to cease.
The Word promises me healing and rest in God's peace.

I asked, but I didn't get - so what's-up with that?
If you loved me Lord you'd give ... Ain't that a fact!

Lord I've asked for understanding, speak to me,
I can't hear your voice, I'm blind and can't see.

-25-

I asked, but I didn't get - so what's-up with that,
If you loved me Lord you'd give … Ain't that a fact!

So what am I doing wrong, that I need to quit,
Is it just that I'm whining, and throwing a fit!

Other Christians are praying and getting blessed,
But my praying is fruitless - my life seems a mess.

I've asked other saints about the truth of Your Word,
And their responses to me seem trite and absurd.

They tell me to repent and ask forgiveness for my sin,
That I'm full of pride, my prayers are blowing in the wind.

They say that when I ask, I ask amiss,
I thought it would be easy – So what's up with this?

They say I need to remember that there is a price,
I should be doing my part, it doesn't count just being nice.

I should forgive others, and repent of my sin,
And recognize that it's by faith, the Father's pleasure, I win.

And obedience is important better than sacrifice,
Getting my will in line and daily laying down my life.

Christians that are doers of the Word,
And have a relationship with Christ – Never crack!

I asked, but I didn't get, so what's-up with that,
If You loved me Lord you'd give – Ain't that a fact!

-26-

It's Alright

James 1:5 (KJV)

I'm like the kid who pesters their mother,
And my father and sisters and even my brother.
Wanting answers to every mysterious wonder,
So many questions – I like to ponder.

I want to know how a tree grows so high?
How many stars are in the sky?
How does a hummingbird really fly?
Mother, mother, please tell me why?

And with the Lord I am just the same,
I pray and pray and call His name.
Wanting answers to problems, clear vision and sight,
But all He says, sometimes is, "It's Alright."

And when I get the "It's Alright," response, it's quite profound,
There is something inside me that settles down.
A peace that floods my very being,
I know the problem is solved without my seeing.

I'm coming to know the Father well,
And about Him to everyone I tell,
About His answers as we talk – that's quite,
Soothing to my Spirit each time I hear, "It's Alright."

Just Wait!

Psalm 27:14, 25:3, 37:18; Isaiah 40:31 (KJV)

I'm tired Lord, I've had enough,
How many times must I learn this lesson of trust.
I learned to trust you when I had that trial,
I was praising Your Name all the while.

Didn't you see the way I handled myself,
I relied on You and trusted in Your wealth.
I lifted my hands and praised your name,
I worked the Word and drove Satan to shame.

So now that I learned that lesson you see,
I'm ready to move on – now go on and bless me!
Bless me with the riches and desires of my heart,
For Your Word promises me prosperity if I've done my part.

But Saints remember it's not you who decides,
When the lesson is learned and when you have arrived.
It's the Father who knows just when you are ready,
It takes many years to learn to trust and be steady.

Steady and sure, immovable and steadfast,
Waiting on the Lord till you think you can't last.
And just when you think you can't go on,
You'll mount like an eagle and be airborne.

He'll give you strength to continue this race,
Because of His love and mercy and grace.
Be still, shut-up, it's not too late,
Learn to rest in Him and – Just Wait!

Dr. Lydia A. Woods

Know Your Enemy

Matthew 4:1-11; Mark 16:17 (KJV)

Come on soldiers, gather round,
We're going to war today on the battleground.

You know the enemy is not very smart,
But he is effective and good at his part.

Let's take the time to get some wisdom here,
My first lesson to you is – never fear!

If you've got the basics about the Father and Son,
Never forget that the battle is already won.

But we must play it out for scripture to be fulfilled,
Take it home to the ending, that will really thrill.

All the Saints and Angelic forces in heaven and earth,
I'm talking about a plan that was forged before your birth.

But it's very important for all Saints to know,
That the enemy is real and to Spiritual warfare go.

For the enemy's weapons are fear and doubt,
He'll try to make you forget what you are all about.

-29-

He'll try to get you to focus the war on your brother,
You'll forget you're commanded to love one another.

He'll make you fearful for your very life,
But remember, you've laid it down, bought with a price.

He doesn't have any new weapons, the old ones work just fine,
For years he's been successful, kicking Saints in the behind.

Satan's plan is simple, it was the same yesterday,
To get you to believe in what he has to say.

Now he continually talks inside your head,
Picking at your weakness and the fears you dread.

The moment you begin to agree with him,
You have sold your birthright and your future is dim.

You've given him power and he can rule,
Over you – so don't be no fool.

Neutralize his weapons ignorance, doubt, confusion and fear,
By using the Name of Jesus on the battlefield frontier!

Lean Not

Proverbs 3:5-6; James 1:5 (KJV)

Lean not to thy own understanding,
For you haven't got all the facts.
Take it from the One who knows all,
For your understanding is feeble and lacks.

It lacks, the wisdom of the ages,
It lacks, because you're not full grown.
It lacks, because your wisdom is fuzzy.
It lacks, because of sin that is sown.

I know you made good grades in school.
You've always been told that you are smart.
But your intellect is no good in this realm,
In the Spirit it's faith that sets you apart.

So take your understanding from the Father,
He is wise and has your best interest at heart,
He knows that you are a child just stumbling,
He is willing to pick you up and take your part.

So lean not to thy own understanding,
Ask for wisdom, He will give it freely to you.
For His thoughts and His ways are much higher,
But it's His understanding that will see you through!

Love is an Action

Philippians 4:19 (KJV)

The Child asked the Mother, "Mommy, do you love me?
You didn't tell me today, where is your love, I just don't see."

My darling child, I told you a hundred times today,
Did you not hear me? - I said, I love you in every way.

I told you, I loved you by waking you up,
In preparing your meals and filling your cup.

In providing the roof, over your head,
By turning on the heat, as you slept in your bed.

By driving you to school, giving lunch money and a kiss,
By giving you a hug, whenever you insist.

In combing your hair, and washing your clothes,
And listening to your tales, of junior high woes.

Helping with your homework, and watching the game that you won,
By telling you no ...till your chores are all done.

For my darling, love isn't just words that you say,
Love is an action that you show every day!

So if you are wondering if God really loves you,
Look at your life and see if it's true.

For you are His darling child, He said, "I love you, today,"
'Cause "Love is An Action" that He shows every day!

So What's-Up With That!

Malachi 3:13-17 (KJV)

Lord, I don't think, Your Word is true,
Because You haven't done what I asked You to.

It's hard for me to believe, what You say,
Because I see no evidence of Your love today.

Your Word said, "To ask and I would receive,"
If I pray and truly in my heart believe.

But that didn't happen, so What's-Up with that!
This Christian, faith thing, seems a bunch of crap!

Lord, don't you know what I have done,
I've forgiven my brothers and sisters, one by one.

I gave to the poor, when I had none,
Blessed my enemies, everyone.

I've sacrificed and been through many trials,
Believing in You all the while.

So What's-Up With this – cause when I knock,
The door doesn't open, it's bolted tight and locked.

I feel like I'm beating my head against a stone wall,
I've cried out in my pain, but You don't hear my call.

You said, to seek and I would find,
But all I get is kicked in my behind.

I cannot see Your love for me,
The sinners seem to be living high and free.

They are not calling on Your name from day to day,
They don't even try to practice what You say.

They're winning the lottery and getting dreams fulfilled,
It looks like I'm going backwards or standing still.

I seemed better off before I knew Your name,
I'm feeling most times that I'm going insane.

So what's-up with Your Word, prove something to me,
Give me a sign of Your love so I can see.

Cause if I had a sign you see,
I could believe in Your love for me! – (Not!)

Dr. Lydia A. Woods

Take Out the Trash!

Ephesians 6:18; James 5:13; I Thessalonians 5:17;
Romans 8:16 (KJV)

The pressure of living on the earth,
Builds to a fever pitch and you wonder if it's worth,
All the hassle and strain, we all need relief,
We need to take it all to the Lord, that's my belief.

For only He can handle all the stress,
Keep us sane under the pressure of all this mess,
Sometimes we forget to give it all to Him, we are remiss,
One day He explained it to me just like this.

How often do you take out your trash,
That's filled with leftovers like corned beef hash,
Rotten tomatoes, meat, and potato peels,
Paper, and bottles – this situation is real!

It's serious business if the trash isn't taken out,
You'd have a serious problem without a doubt.
Do you really want me to describe the mess there would be,
The smell would be out of this world – you see!

Well in the Spirit a process like this exists,
The Spirit fills with trash, now I must insist.
That you "work" with me here as I explain,
This parable that the Lord has put in my brain.

A Collection of Christian Poems   *Take Out the Trash!*

We must dump that garbage from our spirits, 'cause I suspect
It's been building quite some time because of your neglect.
To take the garbage out in a consistent way,
Now admit that you've not been taking it out every day.

You may take out that little trash every now and then,
But the big stuff's been building that – unrepented sin.
Now when I finally can't stand that funky smell in me,
It's to the throne room, I'm running to the arms of thee!

Now the scene is not pretty, these sessions with Him,
Standard equipment is a towel and repentance from sin.
I cry and cry as the Holy Spirit reveals to me my sin,
And shows me the denial that I have been in.

That feeling of God's forgiveness overwhelms and comforts me,
I wipe my tears and now I'm able to see.
That the rotten garbage has now been released,
Revelation begins to flood me and my pain begins to cease.

I have a new walk and a deeper faith when it is done,
"So take out the Trash," often – Give it all to His Son!

Unable to Receive

Luke 6:38; Malachi 3:10 (KJV)

He will pour out a blessing of which you can't conceive.
So big and mighty you can't even receive.

Have you ever had that feeling of "can't even receive,"
You get choked up and can't speak, the tears won't recede.

The blessing is shaken together, running over and pressed down.
There isn't a cup big enough to be found.

That can contain His blessing and love for you,
So just hold on and be blessed – What else can you do?

With Persecution...

Matthew 5:10-12; II Corinthians 4:9-18 (KJV)

Now when you dine at the Lord's table,
He's serving up a meal, fit for a king.
But you better know what's served with redemption,
It's a dish called – *"With Persecution."*

Now of all the dishes served by the Lord,
"With Persecution," is a bitter dish indeed,
And none of His children take pleasure or delight,
In that dish that is served most every night.

The Father insists that – *"With Persecution,"* be served,
That no meal is quite ever complete without,
But His children all moan and groan and pout,
For they question this dish without a doubt.

Why add – *"With Persecution,"* to every meal,
What ingredients are so special inside,
The taste is so darn unpleasant,
Will it grow our hair or make one wise?

-39-

The Father knows that – "*With Persecution,*"
Builds strong Spiritual bones,
Helps our digestion of long-suffering and humble pie,
And after just a little while,
You'll just come to accept it and not question why.

Then slowly you'll begin to understand,
That "*With Persecution,*" is a necessary dish indeed,
That the making of mature Saints is the purpose,
And "*With Persecution,*" helps every Saint to succeed,

In our growing process here on earth,
As we come to understand the purpose of our birth,
Just pass that dish down this way,
I'm going to enjoy me some – "*With Persecution,*" Today!

Scriptural
References

Above All

John 14:13; I John 5:14; Ephesians 3:10 (KJV)

John 14:13 (KJV)
[13] And whatsoever ye shall ask in my name, that will I do, that the Father may be glorified in the Son.

I John 5:14 (KJV)
[14] And this is the confidence that we have in him, that, if we ask any thing according to his will, he heareth us:

Ephesians 3:10 (KJV)
[10] To the intent that now unto the principalities and powers in heavenly places might be known by the church the manifold wisdom of God,

Be Still!

Psalm 46:10 (KJV)

Psalm 46:10 (KJV)
[10] Be still, and know that I am God: I will be exalted among the heathen, I will be exalted in the earth.

Children of the King

I John 3:1, 9; Psalm 91:11; Matthew 4:6 (KJV)

I John 3:1 (KJV)
[1] Behold, what manner of love the Father hath bestowed upon us, that we should be called the sons of God: therefore the world knoweth us not, because it knew him not.

I John 3:9 (KJV)
[9] Whosoever is born of God doth not commit sin; for his seed remaineth in him: and he cannot sin, because he is born of God.

Psalm 91:11 (KJV)
[11] For he shall give his angels charge over thee, to keep thee in all thy ways.

Matthew 4:6 (KJV)
[6] And saith unto him, If thou be the Son of God, cast thyself down: for it is written, He shall give his angels charge concerning thee: and in their hands they shall bear thee up, lest at any time thou dash thy foot against a stone.

Doin' the Adam

Genesis 3:1-24 (KJV)

Genesis 3:1-24 (KJV)

[1] Now the serpent was more subtil than any beast of the field which the LORD God had made. And he said unto the woman, Yea, hath God said, Ye shall not eat of every tree of the garden?

[2] And the woman said unto the serpent, We may eat of the fruit of the trees of the garden:

[3] But of the fruit of the tree which is in the midst of the garden, God hath said, Ye shall not eat of it, neither shall ye touch it, lest ye die.

[4] And the serpent said unto the woman, Ye shall not surely die:

[5] For God doth know that in the day ye eat thereof, then your eyes shall be opened, and ye shall be as gods, knowing good and evil.

[6] And when the woman saw that the tree was good for food, and that it was pleasant to the eyes, and a tree to be desired to make one wise, she took of the fruit thereof, and did eat, and gave also unto her husband with her; and he did eat.

[7] And the eyes of them both were opened, and they knew that they were naked; and they sewed fig leaves together, and made themselves aprons.

[8] And they heard the voice of the LORD God walking in the garden in the cool of the day: and Adam and his wife hid themselves from the presence of the LORD God amongst the trees of the garden.

[9] And the LORD God called unto Adam, and said unto him, Where art thou?

[10] And he said, I heard thy voice in the garden, and I was afraid, because I was naked; and I hid myself.

[11] And he said, Who told thee that thou wast naked? Hast thou eaten of the tree, whereof I commanded thee that thou shouldest not eat?

¹² And the man said, The woman whom thou gavest to be with me, she gave me of the tree, and I did eat.

¹³ And the LORD God said unto the woman, What is this that thou hast done? And the woman said, The serpent beguiled me, and I did eat.

¹⁴ And the LORD God said unto the serpent, Because thou hast done this, thou art cursed above all cattle, and above every beast of the field; upon thy belly shalt thou go, and dust shalt thou eat all the days of thy life:

¹⁵ And I will put enmity between thee and the woman, and between thy seed and her seed; it shall bruise thy head, and thou shalt bruise his heel.

¹⁶ Unto the woman he said, I will greatly multiply thy sorrow and thy conception; in sorrow thou shalt bring forth children; and thy desire shall be to thy husband, and he shall rule over thee.

¹⁷ And unto Adam he said, Because thou hast hearkened unto the voice of thy wife, and hast eaten of the tree, of which I commanded thee, saying, Thou shalt not eat of it: cursed is the ground for thy sake; in sorrow shalt thou eat of it all the days of thy life;

¹⁸ Thorns also and thistles shall it bring forth to thee; and thou shalt eat the herb of the field;

¹⁹ In the sweat of thy face shalt thou eat bread, till thou return unto the ground; for out of it wast thou taken: for dust thou art, and unto dust shalt thou return.

²⁰ And Adam called his wife's name Eve; because she was the mother of all living.

²¹ Unto Adam also and to his wife did the LORD God make coats of skins, and clothed them.

-47-

22 And the LORD God said, Behold, the man is become as one of us, to know good and evil: and now, lest he put forth his hand, and take also of the tree of life, and eat, and live for ever:

23 Therefore the LORD God sent him forth from the garden of Eden, to till the ground from whence he was taken.

24 So he drove out the man; and he placed at the east of the garden of Eden Cherubims, and a flaming sword which turned every way, to keep the way of the tree of life.

Father Knows Best

Proverbs 1:7; James 1:5 (KJV)

Proverbs 1:7 (KJV)
7 The fear of the LORD is the beginning of knowledge: but fools despise wisdom and instruction.

James 1:5 (KJV)
5 If any of you lack wisdom, let him ask of God, that giveth to all men liberally, and upbraideth not; and it shall be given him.

For the Elect's Sake

Mark 13:20 (KJV)

Mark 13:20 (KJV)
[20] And except that the Lord had shortened those days, no flesh should be saved: but for the elect's sake, whom he hath chosen, he hath shortened the days.

Get in the House

Exodus 12:12-14; James 2:12, 18-19 (KJV)

Exodus 12:12-14 (KJV)

12 For I will pass through the land of Egypt this night, and will smite all the firstborn in the land of Egypt, both man and beast; and against all the gods of Egypt I will execute judgment: I am the LORD. 13 And the blood shall be to you for a token upon the houses where ye are: and when I see the blood, I will pass over you, and the plague shall not be upon you to destroy you, when I smite the land of Egypt. 14 And this day shall be unto you for a memorial; and ye shall keep it a feast to the LORD throughout your generations; ye shall keep it a feast by an ordinance for ever.

James 2:12 (KJV)

12 So speak ye, and so do, as they that shall be judged by the law of liberty.

James 2:18-19 (KJV)

18 Yea, a man may say, Thou hast faith, and I have works: shew me thy faith without thy works, and I will shew thee my faith by my works. 19 Thou believest that there is one God; thou doest well: the devils also believe, and tremble.

God's M.O.

I Corinthians 1:26-27, 2:7, 3:19; Luke 2:7; Ephesians 3:5 (KJV)

I Corinthians 1:26-27 (KJV)

[26] For ye see your calling, brethren, how that not many wise men after the flesh, not many mighty, not many noble, are called:

[27] But God hath chosen the foolish things of the world to confound the wise; and God hath chosen the weak things of the world to confound the things which are mighty;

I Corinthians 2:7 (KJV)

[7] But we speak the wisdom of God in a mystery, even the hidden wisdom, which God ordained before the world unto our glory:

I Corinthians 3:19 (KJV)

[19] For the wisdom of this world is foolishness with God. For it is written, He taketh the wise in their own craftiness.

Luke 2:7 (KJV)

[7] And she brought forth her firstborn son, and wrapped him in swaddling clothes, and laid him in a manger; because there was no room for them in the inn.

Ephesians 3:5 (KJV)

[5] Which in other ages was not made known unto the sons of men, as it is now revealed unto his holy apostles and prophets by the Spirit;

I'm Not Lucky - I'm Blessed!

Genesis 12:3, 26:4; Deuteronomy 7:3-14 (KJV)

Genesis 12:3 (KJV)
3 And I will bless them that bless thee, and curse him that curseth thee: and in thee shall all families of the earth be blessed.

Genesis 26:4 (KJV)
4 And I will make thy seed to multiply as the stars of heaven, and will give unto thy seed all these countries; and in thy seed shall all the nations of the earth be blessed;

Deuteronomy 7:3-14 (KJV)
3 Neither shalt thou make marriages with them; thy daughter thou shalt not give unto his son, nor his daughter shalt thou take unto thy son.

4 For they will turn away thy son from following me, that they may serve other gods: so will the anger of the LORD be kindled against you, and destroy thee suddenly.

5 But thus shall ye deal with them; ye shall destroy their altars, and break down their images, and cut down their groves, and burn their graven images with fire.

6 For thou art an holy people unto the LORD thy God: the LORD thy God hath chosen thee to be a special people unto himself, above all people that are upon the face of the earth.

7 The LORD did not set his love upon you, nor choose you, because ye were more in number than any people; for ye were the fewest of all people:

8 But because the LORD loved you, and because he would keep the oath which he had sworn unto your fathers, hath the LORD brought you out with a mighty hand, and redeemed you out of the house of bondmen, from the hand of Pharaoh king of Egypt.

-53-

[9] Know therefore that the L<small>ORD</small> thy God, he is God, the faithful God, which keepeth covenant and mercy with them that love him and keep his commandments to a thousand generations;

[10] And repayeth them that hate him to their face, to destroy them: he will not be slack to him that hateth him, he will repay him to his face.

[11] Thou shalt therefore keep the commandments, and the statutes, and the judgments, which I command thee this day, to do them.

[12] Wherefore it shall come to pass, if ye hearken to these judgments, and keep, and do them, that the L<small>ORD</small> thy God shall keep unto thee the covenant and the mercy which he sware unto thy fathers:

[13] And he will love thee, and bless thee, and multiply thee: he will also bless the fruit of thy womb, and the fruit of thy land, thy corn, and thy wine, and thine oil, the increase of thy kine, and the flocks of thy sheep, in the land which he sware unto thy fathers to give thee.

[14] Thou shalt be blessed above all people: there shall not be male or female barren among you, or among your cattle.

I'm Tired!

John 16:33; Ephesians 5:3-5 (KJV)

John 16:33 (KJV)
[33] These things I have spoken unto you, that in me ye might have peace. In the world ye shall have tribulation: but be of good cheer; I have overcome the world.

Ephesians 5:3-5 (KJV)
[3] But fornication, and all uncleanness, or covetousness, let it not be once named among you, as becometh saints;
[4] Neither filthiness, nor foolish talking, nor jesting, which are not convenient: but rather giving of thanks.
[5] For this ye know, that no whoremonger, nor unclean person, nor covetous man, who is an idolater, hath any inheritance in the kingdom of Christ and of God.

If You Loved Me Lord...

Romans 8:26; James 4:3 (KJV)

Romans 8:26 (KJV)
[26] Likewise the Spirit also helpeth our infirmities: for we know not what we should pray for as we ought: but the Spirit itself maketh intercession for us with groanings which cannot be uttered.

James 4:3 (KJV)
[3] Ye ask, and receive not, because ye ask amiss, that ye may consume it upon your lusts.

It's Alright

James 1:5 (KJV)

James 1:5 (KJV)
[5] If any of you lack wisdom, let him ask of God, that giveth to all men liberally, and upbraideth not; and it shall be given him.

Just Wait!

Psalm 25:3, 27:14, 37:18; Isaiah 40:31 (KJV)

Psalm 25:3 (KJV)
³ Yea, let none that wait on thee be ashamed: let them be ashamed which transgress without cause.

Psalm 27:14 (KJV)
¹⁴ Wait on the LORD: be of good courage, and he shall strengthen thine heart: wait, I say, on the LORD.

Psalm 37:18 (KJV)
¹⁸ The LORD knoweth the days of the upright: and their inheritance shall be for ever.

Isaiah 40:31 (KJV)
³¹ But they that wait upon the LORD shall renew their strength; they shall mount up with wings as eagles; they shall run, and not be weary; and they shall walk, and not faint.

Know Your Enemy

Matthew 4:1-11; Mark 16:17 (KJV)

Matthew 4:1-11 Version (KJV)

[1] Then was Jesus led up of the Spirit into the wilderness to be tempted of the devil.

[2] And when he had fasted forty days and forty nights, he was afterward an hungred.

[3] And when the tempter came to him, he said, If thou be the Son of God, command that these stones be made bread.

[4] But he answered and said, It is written, Man shall not live by bread alone, but by every word that proceedeth out of the mouth of God.

[5] Then the devil taketh him up into the holy city, and setteth him on a pinnacle of the temple,

[6] And saith unto him, If thou be the Son of God, cast thyself down: for it is written, He shall give his angels charge concerning thee: and in their hands they shall bear thee up, lest at any time thou dash thy foot against a stone.

[7] Jesus said unto him, It is written again, Thou shalt not tempt the Lord thy God.

[8] Again, the devil taketh him up into an exceeding high mountain, and sheweth him all the kingdoms of the world, and the glory of them;

[9] And saith unto him, All these things will I give thee, if thou wilt fall down and worship me.

[10] Then saith Jesus unto him, Get thee hence, Satan: for it is written, Thou shalt worship the Lord thy God, and him only shalt thou serve.

[11] Then the devil leaveth him, and, behold, angels came and ministered unto him.

Mark 16:17 (KJV)
[17] And these signs shall follow them that believe; In my name shall they cast out devils; they shall speak with new tongues;

Lean Not

Proverbs 3:5-6; James 1:5 (KJV)

Proverbs 3:5-6 (KJV)
5 Trust in the LORD with all thine heart; and lean not unto thine own understanding.
6 In all thy ways acknowledge him, and he shall direct thy paths.

James 1:5 (KJV)
5 If any of you lack wisdom, let him ask of God, that giveth to all men liberally, and upbraideth not; and it shall be given him.

Love is an Action

Philippians 4:19 (KJV)

Philippians 4:19 (KJV)

[19] But my God shall supply all your need according to his riches in glory by Christ Jesus.

So What's-Up With That!

Malachi 3:13-17 (KJV)

Malachi 3:13-17 (KJV)

¹³ Your words have been stout against me, saith the LORD. Yet ye say, What have we spoken so much against thee?

¹⁴ Ye have said, It is vain to serve God: and what profit is it that we have kept his ordinance, and that we have walked mournfully before the LORD of hosts?

¹⁵ And now we call the proud happy; yea, they that work wickedness are set up; yea, they that tempt God are even delivered.

¹⁶ Then they that feared the LORD spake often one to another: and the LORD hearkened, and heard it, and a book of remembrance was written before him for them that feared the LORD, and that thought upon his name.

¹⁷ And they shall be mine, saith the LORD of hosts, in that day when I make up my jewels; and I will spare them, as a man spareth his own son that serveth him.

Take Out the Trash!

Ephesians 6:18; James 5:13; I Thessalonians 5:17;
Romans 8:16 (KJV)

Ephesians 6:18 (KJV)
18 Praying always with all prayer and supplication in the Spirit, and watching thereunto with all perseverance and supplication for all saints;

James 5:13 (KJV)
13 Is any among you afflicted? let him pray. Is any merry? let him sing psalms.

I Thessalonians 5:17 (KJV)
17 Pray without ceasing.

Romans 8:16 (KJV)
16 The Spirit itself beareth witness with our spirit, that we are the children of God:

Unable to Receive

Luke 6:38; Malachi 3:10 (KJV)

Luke 6:38 (KJV)
[38] Give, and it shall be given unto you; good measure, pressed down, and shaken together, and running over, shall men give into your bosom. For with the same measure that ye mete withal it shall be measured to you again.

Malachi 3:10 (KJV)
[10] Bring ye all the tithes into the storehouse, that there may be meat in mine house, and prove me now herewith, saith the LORD of hosts, if I will not open you the windows of heaven, and pour you out a blessing, that there shall not be room enough to receive it.

With Persecution...

Matthew 5:10-12; II Corinthians 4:9-18 (KJV)

Matthew 5:10-12 (KJV)
[10] Blessed are they which are persecuted for righteousness' sake: for theirs is the kingdom of heaven.

[11] Blessed are ye, when men shall revile you, and persecute you, and shall say all manner of evil against you falsely, for my sake.

[12] Rejoice, and be exceeding glad: for great is your reward in heaven: for so persecuted they the prophets which were before you.

II Corinthians 4:9-18 (KJV)
[9] Persecuted, but not forsaken; cast down, but not destroyed;

[10] Always bearing about in the body the dying of the Lord Jesus, that the life also of Jesus might be made manifest in our body.

[11] For we which live are always delivered unto death for Jesus' sake, that the life also of Jesus might be made manifest in our mortal flesh.

[12] So then death worketh in us, but life in you.

[13] We having the same spirit of faith, according as it is written, I believed, and therefore have I spoken; we also believe, and therefore speak;

[14] Knowing that he which raised up the Lord Jesus shall raise up us also by Jesus, and shall present us with you.

[15] For all things are for your sakes, that the abundant grace might through the thanksgiving of many redound to the glory of God.

[16] For which cause we faint not; but though our outward man perish, yet the inward man is renewed day by day.

[17] For our light affliction, which is but for a moment, worketh for us a far more exceeding and eternal weight of glory;

-66-

[18] While we look not at the things which are seen, but at the things which are not seen: for the things which are seen are temporal; but the things which are not seen are eternal.

Scriptural Index